Never, Never, Never Give Up!

By

Christine R. Dyer

Leave No Sister Behind™ Publications
Gulfport, MS

Never, Never, Never Give Up!

Copyright © 2008 by Christine R. Dyer
Never, Never, Never Give Up!

All rights reserved solely by Author

No part of this book may be reproduced without written permission of the Publisher.

Bible quotations are taken from the Holy Bible, New International Version®. Copyright ©1973, 1978,1984 by International Bible Society. Used by permission of Zondervan. All rights reserved.

Printed in the United States of America
ISBN-13: 978-0-9787004-0-9

Editor: Carol Givner
Cover Design: Celesta Caston

www.LeaveNoSisterBehind.com

For the love of my life,
Ronald J Dyer, Sr.
Thanks for taking over my chores while I worked at the computer.

My three children:
Latasha, Ronald Jr, and Latreace
My son-in-law, Troy
Daughter in-law, Keturah

Grandchildren:
Brianna, Jessica, Michael,
Mariah, Makalya, Demetrius,
Durius, Justice, Jayden
Michael, Micah, Shawn,
Keshawn, Jordan and Godchildren

My Mother
Ernestine

Never, Never, Never Give Up!

For

———————————————————————

From

———————————————————————

Date

——————————————

Preface

I am reminded of the woman in the Bible who was sick for twelve long years. She had a continuous flow of blood, and spent all of her money on many doctors with the expectation of becoming healed. At some point in her life, she heard about Jesus being a healer; with great anticipation, she thought she would try what He had to offer since man had failed to deliver her hope.

One day she found herself pressing in a hostile crowd where Jesus was passing by. Her determination caused her to make a connection that would change her life forever—as well as her condition. Just by touching the hem of Jesus' garment, she received her healing (Luke 8:43-48).

I am sure her body was weak, as it had suffered a great loss of blood; although obstacles were in the way, she never stopped pressing. Her mind was determined to let nothing stop her, and her faith and persistence caused her to receive her long awaited desire.

We must have the same persistence in our lives, believing beyond what we see in the natural. Moreover, we must learn never to give up until our change comes.

This leads me to share a personal story about a persistent prayer concerning my father. He was a man who was firm about his belief, sharp in the Word and a soul winner with a sold-out heart to God. He would witness to people and they would end up giving their lives to Christ. He would pray for them and encourage them to live.

My father would go out of his way for anyone who needed help. I knew well that he practiced what he taught others and I respected him for being a man of his word.

Out of seven siblings, I was the oldest of five brothers and two sisters. Raised in a Christian home, my father taught us many things. Particularly, he taught us love, although there were never any discussions about it, his demonstration proved more powerful than words. When we spent time together, we would sit attentively at the interesting things he told us.

To my surprise, I saw a drastic change in my father's actions; he stopped visiting the church, and made no mention of God. God became less and less a part of his life as he began to follow the things of the world, from hanging out to being the life of everyone's party.

Although church was no longer a part of his life, he made sure we continued doing what was right. Nevertheless, it seems as though our family structure started crumbling because of his erroneous decisions. They affected us all—I believe, even my mother. I could imagine the displeasure and disappointment that my mother might have experienced at that time. Prior to his change, I always admired what my parents had as a couple; in fact, I desired to have a marriage like their marriage when I grew up. Their togetherness created an atmosphere of peace, love and happiness for the family. Unfortunately, when he left Christ, things changed.

    I can remember having dreams about my father dying in the hospital. Every time, I would wake up crying. I finally got up the nerves to call my father and tell him about it. He replied, "It was only a dream." He tried to console me, but it was to no avail. Since I was serious about heaven, this dream alarmed me to go to God on his behalf and cry out for his soul. While pleading to God, I reminded Him of all the wonderful things my father had done before he turned his back on Him. I told him about how my father had diligently taught us of His word. I shared how my father had witnessed and brought many souls to the kingdom of God. I prayed for God to change his heart before his soul ended up in an undesirable place—eternal damnation.

Time went by, and there was no evidence of change as far as the eye could see. In spite of this, I continued to press into God's presence. It was like a child pleading to the Father for her father. My pleas ultimately turned into a persistent, desperate cry. I knew I could not make God do anything, but I could ask that He consider sparing my father's soul since he had spared his life many times before. My concern was for God not to allow him to leave this earth without Him in his life.

Again, I went back to the throne to build upon my case that which concerned my father. I begin to tell God that He was a faithful Christian when he was in church, and when he witnessed to people, they would give their lives to God. I could not fail to mention the time when some of our relatives came from out of town and moved in with us. After my father witnessed to them about the goodness of Jesus, they found themselves going to church.

Even though my father was sick most of his life, he did not allow his circumstances to dictate his attitude. He was a fighter at heart, and steadily stayed the course in teaching us how to live a Christian life. He would say, "What you are now, you are now becoming." I did not want to hear what he was saying at the time. Furthermore, I often wondered *how he could chastise me when he was not living right.*

I remember crying myself to sleep because I felt that other things were taking our place, as our father was getting further away from us. I had to learn to live a Godly life without being judgmental and angry because my father made a choice to do things his way.

As I matured in God, I became an intense prayer warrior making up in my mind that my father was not going to be lost—even if it meant praying for him on his deathbed.

Well, one day my father had gotten very ill and had to be admitted to the hospital. The doctor called me into the room to tell me that my father might not live long. I looked at my mother and said, "He's been sick before and always came through." I just did not believe he was dying at the time. I was too determined not to let him go without his salvation; thus, I continued in prayer.

Later, after his recovery, there was still no change, which puzzled me because if I were that close to death, I would have ran to God.

On one occasion, I drove up to the doctor's office as they wheeled him into an ambulance because of a heart attack. I heard him whistling a tune, but the moment he saw me, he stopped and calmly said that he would be all right. Then, he assured me that he would be home soon. Again, he recovered—without change. Yet, I continued to believe.

This particular day—a day I would never forget—my Aunt Lue and her friends (Pastor Allen from Florida and Pastor Doris from Boston) came to visit my dad. I believe these women were on a mission. Upon entering the house, they exchanged hellos and asked if they could come in and pray for him since he had been sick. Graciously, he accepted. Usually, he refused to accept prayer and anyone that would try to persuade him to do differently.

There was an instant transformation within my father after he received their prayers. He raised his hands and began to praise and thank God with tears flowing from his eyes. Everyone in the room was crying. I knew he had changed before my eyes because where darkness had been trying to overthrow his soul, light had overcome it. Literally, I saw his face change to a lighter color.

Pastor Allen began to talk to him. She asked, "How do you feel?" He replied, "Great." Then she told him that while she was praying for him, she had received a word from the Lord: he did not have long to live on this earth. He said that he understood what she was saying. He did not deviate from the way he was feeling; the peace of God remained upon his face. I felt rather joyous in my spirit —despite her words from the Lord— because God had shown him grace and mercy. He could have died in sin.

I feel that the prayers we pray in life are not in vain. All we have to do is stay focused, be determined, believe beyond what we see in the natural, and never give up on our dream, our goals, and our visions. I pondered on what Pastor Allen had said about my father having a short time to live. We had no idea that three days later (after my father had given his life back to Christ) he would die.

My Aunt Daisy (my father's sister) came to visit that day. I believed she was there by divine appointment. They were talking and he said that he could not see; consequently, he closed his eyes and slept on into heaven. Every time sadness tried to arise, *peace* would remind me that my father came back to Christ.

One final day, I received a call that my father was in the hospital. When I arrived, the Chaplain greeted me at the door. I knew in my heart that he was gone. I asked if I could see him by myself, and he consented. I walked in the room and saw peace upon his face. I never questioned the Lord as to why He had taken my father; Instead, I told God, "Thank You."

I had vowed never to give up until he turned back to God. At the funeral, I cried, but I could also feel God's strength as I viewed his body for the last time. It appeared that some people were watching and waiting for me to fall apart. All I could think about was the fact that God kept his promise. Some would say, "If God is God, why did he die?" I say that God is God because He answered my prayer.

Who are you praying for? Who are you standing in the gap for? Do not give up. Maybe you have spent years in prayer for them. Until you see a change, keep praying. Just because you see no evidence of change, understand that something is happening in the spirit realm. Don't be distracted by what it "appears" to be in the natural (that which you see with the natural eye). Remember that my father's deliverance did not come over night. So, never, never, never, give up.

--Christine R. Dyer

Table of Contents

Diamonds in the Sky 15

There Is Hope! 17

Working for My Good 19

Come to the Mercy Seat! 21

Storms 23

Bless Him at All Times 25

Who Told You? 27

It Shall Come to Pass 29

Put Me Back Together 31

Are You Ready! 33

I Shall Live and Not Die! 35

Joy 39

What About Prayer! 41

Sold Out to God! 45

Reality Check 47

It's Yours 49

I Can't Take It Anymore 51

Why Me? 53

Who Do You Belong To? 55

A Worshiper 57

He Decided to Die 61

The Day of Rest 63

I Am The Head 65

A Love That Never Fails 67

Where Am I? 69

It is Finished 71

Chapter 1

Diamonds in the Sky

Psalms 8:3

As I gazed up to heaven, looking at the stars, I saw they were shining so brightly that I could imagine God gave His command for them just to be, and look beautiful like diamonds in the sky, until He tells them to disappear.

Heaven seems to be quiet tonight. Darkness has overtaken the sun. They're all doing their jobs. The stars and the moon are all waiting on God's command.

If only we could be like the stars, the moon. Just shine in the presence of God and wait for his instructions to do His will.

Never, Never, Never Give Up!

Everything God created has a purpose—even the stars shining like diamonds in the sky.

Chapter 2

There Is Hope!

Turbulent times will tell you there is no hope! Well, there is good news. Jesus said that He came that we may have life and more abundantly. My sister, my brother, be encouraged, because Jesus has already conquered these things. No matter what you're facing, there is hope and Jesus loves you, no matter what you've done. It doesn't matter who you are or what you have done in life, God wants to forgive you; He loves you.

I want to encourage you on today to look up and live—it's going to be all right. Give God your heart if you haven't done so. You may ask, "Evangelist Dyer, how do I do that?" You may not know how to reach God in prayer. Well, we didn't come in this world knowing how to pray, either. All you have to do is be real with God. Take your boxing gloves off. You don't have to fight to get what you need. Tell God about what's concerning you, although He already knows what your situation is. He wants you to tell him...it develops communication. Tell Him you want to change. Talk to Him just as if you're talking to me. Tell Him you want a new life. Ask Him to come into your heart; He promised not to leave you. Maybe you have had a hard time trusting people; maybe you've been hurt or abused by someone you loved, and as a result you guard your heart to protect yourself. Let go and give your heart to God. He will not hurt you. He will heal you from the inside out. There is hope. Allow Him to come to your rescue.

Chapter 3

Working for My Good

Romans 8:28

There were so many days and nights that I cried my eyes out because of what was happening to me. I could not understand why! The bible says that all things work together for the good of those who love God, to those who are the called according to His purpose. At the time, I could not see it.

The older generation would sing a song with words like, "We would understand things by and by." Well, my by and by came. As I matured and grew in knowledge in the word of God, I understood more about the challenges I was facing.

I stopped feeling sorry for myself and was soon delivered from the "why me" syndrome. I made a decision to hold on to God's words and as a result, I found myself becoming strong. The rougher the times got, the more I learned to lean on God. Whenever the enemy tried to form a weapon against me, not only did it fail to prosper, but God turned the situation around for my good.

It was always in my favor. Always working for my good.

Chapter 4

Come to the Mercy Seat!

God is at the mercy seat. He has plenty of grace and mercy for you. He invites you to come; it is not too late. He already paid the price on Cavalry.

God saw you afar off. He sees your potential. Are you broken? God sees you as whole. He Loves you and wants the best for you.

You are never too far from his reach. Reach out and grab His extended hands of love. It doesn't matter who you are, where you came from or what you've done in life. He is always ready to forgive, heal and accept His creation.

Come to the mercy seat. Don't be afraid. Do come with an open heart to receive joy and peace. He'll bless you and your family.

Please come. Come with words—talk to God, and be real with Him. Tell Him what you need.

Ask Him to change you. Tell Him you're sorry for your sins. Then, thank Him for grace and mercy.

Go from there and find you a bible-believing church where you can grow and flourish in the word of God.

You can be all that God has declared you to be.

Chapter 5

Storms

Psalm 46:1-7

Though the storms keep on raging in our lives, we have a hope in God that it will not always be this way. God is going to turn the storms in a different direction.

I've been in the storms of life, and God has always come to my rescue. The important thing I had to remember was that if He did it for me before, he'll do it again. We must keep the faith and remember God's word. Storms are funny sometimes, because they come in different ways—a little rain, sometimes with hail, sometimes with lightning, sometimes thunder.

They can be fierce; they can tear you apart, but as long as you hold on to God's hand in the storm, they will not overtake you. God said in His word the water will not overflow you.

Hold on to Him, and He won't let go of you. There is calmness and peace after the storm, and sometimes that's how it is in our lives. Storms; then peace after the storm.

Chapter 6

Bless Him at All Times

Psalm 34

Can you say, "I will bless the Lord at all times?"

Can you say, "I will bless the Lord when bills are facing me, and I can't see any finances coming in?"

Can you say, "I will bless the Lord when my marriage is falling apart, and I know I have done everything there is to do to make it work?"

Can you say, "I will bless the Lord when my children have gone astray, and I taught and raised them to do the right thing, and they do the opposite?"

Can you say, "I will bless the Lord when people turn their backs on me when I went out of my way to help them?"

Even in my tears, in my loneliest moments, I've found time to thank God. I bless Him.

Sometimes I don't understand why we must go through life's ups and downs, but I've learned to trust God, knowing that He will bring me out of whatever I'm facing.

So even on your worst day, you can say, "I will bless the Lord at all times. His praise shall continually be in my mouth!"

Chapter 7

Who Told You?

Isaiah 40: 31

Who told you that you could not make it? Have you been listening to that Deceiver?

The Liar wants you to accept defeat. The Destroyer wants you erased from the picture of the kingdom of God.

The Ancient one wants to feed you lies as he has always done from the beginning of time. You are chosen. You are more than a conqueror. Simply royalty.

Shake the dust from your feet and walk in your destiny. Go on to perfection and refuse to stand still.

Never, Never, Never Give Up!

Never, ever allow your circumstances to dictate to you who you are, where you are going and what you can or can (not) do.

The enemy may have told you that you could not make it, but know that he has whispered the same thought in the ears of every determined soul.

The word of God came back to my remembrance: Those that wait upon the Lord shall renew their strength. They shall mount up with wings as eagles, run, and not grow weary. They shall walk and not faint.

I choose to believe the word of the Lord.

Chapter 8

It Shall Come to Pass

2 Corinthians 1:20

Every word that comes from the mouth of God, shall come to pass. Wait on the promise. It shall come to pass. He will wipe away your tears. It shall come to pass (Rev 21: 4). If God says He'll keep you in perfect peace, then believe Him; He'll do just what He says. It will come to pass.

If you confess your sins, He is faithful and just to forgive us of our sins and cleanse us from all unrighteousness (1 John 1:9). If He said we are forgiven, then we are.

If He said that we are overcomers and shall inherit all things, and He will be our God and we shall be His sons, then we are. Never doubt any prophesy that comes from God. Even though it seems impossible to man and it seems a long time coming, it shall come to pass. God is true to his word.

It seems as if some gifts and visions are locked up...never to be released. They will inevitably become a reality. Don't doubt; keep your faith. Your faith is the substance of things hoped for, the evidence of things not seen.

Every word, every dream, every hope, every anticipation shall come to pass. Tell yourself daily that it shall come to pass. Many years may have come and gone and nothing has happened, but God has his own timing. When your time comes, no one can stop it. What is for you, it is for you. God keeps His promises.

Chapter 9

Put Me Back Together

There is a place in all of us where no one can see. We have on our mask, our disguise. We smile, but deep down inside we have hurts and disappointments in our hearts that say, "I need someone to love, and someone to love me."

Sometimes we don't know how to come to God with our issues, because we've been abused, we've been cast down, we've been forsaken, we've been lied on and lied to. We put up walls, we just exist, we're like a dead man walking, we're numb. We don't feel. You don't have to continue to fall apart because of the hand that life has dealt you.

We need God's touch; God can put you back together again, better than you were before. We have issues, we have problems, we have anger, and we are in pieces. The word of God says, "Come unto to me all that are heavy laden, heavy burdens I will give you rest."

Come, take your mask off; show God the real you. Give Him your heart. He'll give you beauty for your ashes; go ahead run, run, run to Him. Come boldly to the throne of God. You're going to be victorious.

You're going to be a conqueror and rise above your situations; above despair when He puts you back together again.

You don't want to be where you were, you need to go beyond. He'll want to show you a more excellent way of doing things. If you lost your way, you can never go too far where God can't reach you. Let go and let God guide you.

Chapter 10

Are You Ready!

We're living in a time where people have taken their minds off the coming of the Lord. We're so busy. If the Rapture of the Lord came, we may think it's a terrorist attack. We probably wouldn't have a clue, because of all the things that are happening in our world—power outages; planes running into buildings; floods; tornadoes; children, men, and women murdered.

We have gotten numb to what's going on around us. We have lost touch with God. We have allowed the enemy to take our mind off the coming of the Lord. We've forgotten that there will be a major happening that's going to take place in our world. Don't get caught up in the cares of life until you forget what God's word says, that He's coming.

It's the enemy's job to keep us so busy that we have no time for God and no time to go to church. We're working seven days a week, no time to pray, no time to ask God to forgive us, no time to teach our children. The TVs, the videos games, the I-pods, and cell phones have the attention of our children. We can't talk to them, because these things have them caught up in the cares of this life.

No man knows the day and time. Have you made plans, or will you think it's a terrorist attack. We can't wait until the last minute to get ready, so make preparations. If you're not ready, ask Jesus to come into your heart. Ask Him to change you. Find a Bible-believing church where they preach the truth. Tomorrow is not promised to you. Furthermore, the next minute is not promised. But while you are still breathing, it's never too late to reach out for His hand.

Get up! Get ready, be ready, stay ready! Look up and live, for the coming of the Lord draweth nigh.

Chapter 11

I Shall Live and Not Die!

Psalm 118:17

Did you ever feel you weren't going to live to see you next birthday? Well, at the time I did. I'd had many challenges in my health, but God always came and touched my body.

I was determined to achieve in life what God had for me to do for the Kingdom of God.

I had just preached a Sunday morning service. My message was "Too Legit to Quit." I was on a spiritual high, praising God. The service was high, and God blessed the people in the service.

Never think you're not going to be tested to what and about you testify. The next day, I was rushed to the hospital by ambulance; they said that they thought I'd had a heart attack.

The nurses and doctors were all running around; I was stuck with needles; I had an oxygen mask on; it seemed I was going in and out of consciousness. Even if I wasn't sick, by the time the nurses got through with me, I would have been sick. Nevertheless, as I was lying on the stretcher, the message that I preached came to my mind asking me if I was still too legit to quit? I began to cry. What was this all about? See, I had to get focused, because if I didn't watch it, I could find myself having a pity party, asking God why did this have to happen to me? I serve Him.

In spite of this, with tears streaming down my face, I began to raise my hand to God. I was thanking Him for giving me strength to go through what I was going through—although the nurse probably thought I was delirious.

So with my hands lifted up, I began to declare to the enemy that I was still too legit to quit. Then I confessed, "I shall live and not die; I will declare the works of the Lord." God wasn't through with me yet. I still had so many people I had to reach. I had to tell them about the goodness of Jesus and how He empowered my life.

When you are called to the front lines to encourage people, to lift people out of despair, you got to be determined, because the enemy will come at you like a roaring lion. But guess what? The enemy can't destroy you.

You got to believe in your God when your back is up against the wall. He will come to your rescue. Throw your hands up and praise God in the midst of your circumstances. Confuse the enemy! Make Him wonder what's going on with your praising God.

Never, Never, Never Give Up!

Chapter 12

Joy
Psalms 30:5

In case you didn't know it, joy belongs to you! God has given it to us, but the cares of life are always trying to take it.

Anger wants it.
Depression wants it.
Low self-esteem wants it.
Bitterness wants it.
Strife wants it.
Hatred wants it.
But guess who it belongs to?
You!

Never, Never, Never Give Up!

Chapter 13

What About Prayer!

Matthew 21:21-22

It is the enemy's plan to eliminate prayer from the people of God and take away our spiritual weapons. We need to know how to wage war against the enemy through prayer.

Now let us find out what is prayer? It is communing or talking to God. You do not have to rehearse what you are saying; your words come from the heart just as if you are talking to another person.

You might say, "How do I say what I need to say to God?" Example: Lord, I do not know how to pray, but I am coming to you the only way I know how. Please show me the way. The Bible says that we can come boldly to the throne of God. You do not have to be afraid that you will say the wrong thing. We did not all come in the body of Christ knowing how to pray. We must grow in Christ (spiritually) just as we grow in the natural. No one comes out of the womb talking, but as the understanding increases, so does our vocabulary. Do not expect to know all the right things to say when you first start out praying. However, do understand that as your relationship grows with the Lord, so does the language of a prayer. When you pray, you must be in expectation looking for God to answer you.

Prayer changes circumstances, prayer changes you. Prayer is like dynamite, it blows things asunder. It blows your mind when God answers your prayers.

What magnitude of things that can change through prayer. We are told by the word of God that we can cast down imaginations and arguments. Prayer brings peace to your home. Prayer can bring healing; prayer can cause you to have a second chance at life. Even when you are unable to pray, someone else can pray these things into existence for you.

Prayer is an awesome thing. I have so many testimonies about how God answered prayers. One in particular concerned my father. The saints' prayers moved God to intervene on his behalf. At times, it did not look as if he were changing. Actually, it looked impossible, but God granted our request. You have to pray as if someone's life depends on it. This may require intense prayer. Nevertheless, stand steady. Unmovable, never giving up.

Wait on God to answer, because He has timing. If we are going to be effective in our lives, then we must develop a prayer life. Develop a relationship with God through prayer.

Some of us, when we were developing a relationship with someone we admired, we wanted to talk on the phone with that person for breakfast, lunch, and dinner. As that relationship developed, maybe we wanted to tell that person that we loved them. Everyone is different in his or her relationships. So it is with the prayer life.

Some may talk to God only when they need Him, but when you spend time with Him, you want to tell Him how much you love Him, because you have a relationship with Him and not because you want something from Him.

The more you want to know about Jesus, the closer you get to Him. Then you feel you can release your prayer language. You began to

Never, Never, Never Give Up!

reverence Him for who He is; you began to humble yourself before Him. Sometimes you may pray for hours or days on hand and see nothing change; But when you do, you learn not to doubt Him, but trust in his timing. You got to believe in your God.

The enemy's plan is now to stop you from praying, because he knows if the prayer warrior gets loose, he has trouble on his hands. Ephesians 6:10 ; Hebrew 4:16.

Chapter 14

Sold Out to God!

Are we sold out?
Are we committed?
Do we have time for God?
Did we forget our original purpose?
Did we forget our destiny?
Did we lose focus on the call of God.
Are we really sold out to God?
We may say we're sold out, but are we really?
What are our motives for what we do?
Does God play an important part in our lives?
Are we putting Him first? As the Bible says: "Seek Him first and all these things shall be added unto us.
Are we caught up in the material things of this world?
Do we love God as we say we do?

Are we using our God-given gifts to help someone less fortunate than us?

Are we sharing the Gospel of Jesus Christ with others?

Are we really sold out to God?

Are we just numb from everyday living?

Have we lost our joy?

Are we delighting ourselves in the Lord?

Have we forgiven others?

Have we lost our passion for the words of God?

Let's check ourselves. We must ask God to direct our path to:

Forgive others.

Forgive ourselves.

Let go of the past.

Delight ourselves in the Lord.

Restore our passion for the word of God.

Restore our peace.

Renew our passion for reaching souls who are lost as we were. Then we can truly be sold out to God.

Chapter 15

Reality Check

Philippians 3:13-17

There may come a time when your husband or your wife may come to you and say, "I do not want to be with you anymore. I do not want to worship Christ anymore." You have to be strong in God in order not to leave God, or lose your mind. That can be a blow to your marriage, your integrity, your self-esteem, and your whole world.

If it happens, take a reality check and ask yourself this one question: Is this really happening to me? However, know that God is still with you.

When the storm comes, you can stand your ground. Do not let anyone persuade you to do things differently from what you know. It seems as though there is so much violence and fighting and devouring one another—mothers against daughters, and sons against fathers. Everything goes on TV. Some have strayed and lost their morals. Children have gone astray by murdering and being murdered.

Sometimes we feel like saying, "What's the use?" We cannot give up now, as we have to hold on to what we know and what we believe in. We have to know what is right, no matter how ancient it seems to other people.

We have to believe God's words.
He said in his word that things will get this way, but we, the believers, must continue no matter what we see or hear.

Many people started out with us in the faith, but ended up falling by the wayside. We must be the majority and continue. God has been good to you and me. We cannot let our fleshly desires for this world overtake us.

Our trials and tribulations get the best of us sometimes, but remember this: We have a God who is able to keep us in perfect peace despite what is going on around us.

Chapter 16

It's Yours

2 Corinthians 1:20

Has God promised you something in His Word, and it seems as if it's not coming to pass?

If God said He was going to restore your health, your marriage, your finances, etc., believe Him, because His Word is true. Just because you see no signs of things happening for the time being, doesn't mean they're not going to happen.

Don't entertain the thought that it's not going to happen. Satan will paint you a picture of the past. You have to look past failures, hurts, and disappointments, and look beyond what you see. Activate your faith. God's Word says that all of his promises are yes and amen. Look for your blessing everyday; it's already done.

Start thanking Him for doing what He has already said. When you began to praise Him, the enemy is going to take a second look. He's going to say, "Why is s(he) praising God? Nothing good is happening to them. I've given them sickness, diseases, disappointments. I've caused friends and love ones to turn their backs on them. I've caused husbands and wives to be divided and children to go astray."

See, the enemy doesn't like praise. He doesn't understand why you're still praising God in the midst of trials and tribulations, storms, and tornadoes that have been turned loose in your life. And there you still stand with yet another praise on the inside of you. Praise Him, regardless of the circumstances, because He's God. If you must, while you stand in the storm with tears streaming down your cheeks, tell God that you believe and trust Him.

If the Word of God promised you something, I want you to look for it. Don't doubt it, it's yours.

Chapter 17

I Can't Take It Anymore

Isaiah 40:29-31

Do the words *I can't take it anymore* sound familiar? How many times have these words crashed down in front of you? It seems as though the enemy has nailed you to the wall, and he's throwing darts at you, pushing you to the limit.

You've had the same temptation before, but you went through it. The Bible says God gives power to the weak. Are you feeling weak right about now?

If you wait upon the Lord, He shall renew your strength. You shall mount up with wings of eagles. You shall run and not be weary. You shall walk and not faint.

So when you say that you can't take it anymore, you have just given God the opportunity to work for you. Be strong in the Lord and put on the whole armor of God, because the devil is as a roaring lion.

Satan will try to blind what God's word says to us. The Bible says that we have the power to tread over serpents and scorpions and over all the power of the enemy and that nothing by any means shall hurt us. Believe these words!

Also believe this: You can do all things through Jesus Christ, who strengthens you.

Chapter 18

Why Me?

1 CORINTHIANS 1:24-30

Did you ever ask, "Why me?" Well, why not you? Sometimes when we are called to do a job for God, the first thing we think is, *I am not qualified to do the work.* Probably the next thought that appears is something like, *Who am I?* Then we start making excuses why we can't do the job.

Maybe sometimes our self-esteem is not up to the level where it should be, or we have listened to negative people so long that we keep rehearsing their words over and over in our minds.

Get out of the "why me" syndrome! You're special to God. Do the job He has called you to do, however big or small. Don't try to do someone else's job—only what God has called you to do.

Every job is important in the kingdom, whether it's cleaning the church, teaching Sunday school, or ushering people to their seats. All of these positions are important to God. Not everyone has the same calling and ministries, but whatever you are called to do, do it unto the Glory of God. God is depending on you.

Chapter 19

Who Do You Belong To?

I Corinthians 6:20

Why do you live beneath your privileges? Why do you live as if you belong to the Devil? Obviously, you do not know whom you belong to.

You were bought with a price; therefore, glorify God in your body and spirit, which is the temple of God.

Go ahead… tie your spiritual shoes, and walk the walk because you are a child of God!

Now you know, that you know, who you belong to.

Never, Never, Never Give Up!

Chapter 20

A Worshiper

The word *worship* is derived from a word meaning to prostate oneself; to bow down, paying reverence.

I would like to submit my definition of *worship*. Worship is praising God for allowing me to come into His presence, with all of my insecurities, pain, wounds, "why's," and "how-long's."

For many years, I didn't want to serve Him, because I really didn't know who He was. But God didn't give up on me. He put all of my sins in the sea of forgetfulness and saw me, for me—the real me. Before I ever knew who I was or was about, He knew me and everything about me. As I began to serve this Omniscient God, I became a true worshiper. I found myself making contact with Him and finding a new and meaningful relationship with the true and living God.

The more I got into His joyous presence, the more I loved Him, adored Him, and trusted in Him.

There are times when you need not say a word when you come in His presence.

What is a true worshiper? I believe there are conditions for being a true worshiper. The Bible says those who worship must worship in spirit and truth.

This means something is required on your part. "Why?" you ask. Because you're going in the presence of a Holy God. You're taking off your mask:

- You can't live like the Devil and be a true worshiper. God wants truthfulness.
- A true worshiper looks beyond what people think.
- A true worshiper has God's spirit, which is born of the water and spirit.
- A true worshiper has God's character; you identify with his suffering.
- A true worshiper worships Him for who He is and for His unconditional love, knowing we did nothing to deserve it.

- A true worshiper will worship no matter how or from where the storm of life comes.
- A true worshiper will make sacrifices even when s(he) doesn't see the way, understanding that God is the way.
- Worshipers will get in the presence of God with tears streaming down their faces; they're not concerned at this point with how they look.

Are you a worshiper? I wasn't. Didn't know what I was missing. Do you let God see the real you from your standpoint? I didn't. I had a smile on my face, but inside I hurt. However, He already knew the real me.

Are you truthful with Him? I wasn't. I kept saying that I was going to get myself together. Do you make excuses for not coming into His presence—into the inner courts? I did. I didn't feel I was worthy to enter the sacred chambers. Haven't you stayed out of the outer court to long? I did. To this day, I realized I wasted too much time. Are there some things you have to lay down in your life to be a worshiper? I did. I had to lay aside the things that displeased God.

The Father is seeking a true worshiper to worship and that's you, because He loves you. Let

Never, Never, Never Give Up!

Him develop you to be a true worshiper. I did, and He is still doing it.

Chapter 21

He Decided to Die

The song said that He would not come down from the cross. He decided to die just to save us—a people who reject Him, reject his word, and worship other gods. A people who have gone astray. But His fate had already been chosen long ago. He did it so we could be set free from our sins, free from our issues, free from our doubts, and free of our fears.

Why did you do it, Jesus? It was love. Oh, it was unconditional love. He saw us far off and decided to die. They hung Him high, stretched Him wide, and He still didn't see fit to come down off that rugged cross. He decided to die, just to save me, to save you—and yes, if it were only you.

Never, Never, Never Give Up!

Chapter 22

The Day of Rest

REVELATION 21:1-8

When will we have the day of rest from trials and tribulations?
When will the enemy be subdued?
When will the backbiters, mockers, and accusers stop?
 When will the liars stop lying?
When will the children stop going stray?
When will the drugs dealers stop dealing drugs?
When will the murders stop murdering?
When will God say, "Enough?"
The Judgment, the final call, the promise of the Kingdom to God's people.
The great day of rest.

Never, Never, Never Give Up!

Chapter 23

I Am The Head

I am the head and not the tail. These words must I remember when I am feeling low; when people revile me; when I am told I can't stand, I can't make it, I can't take it.

I am God's child! I am the head and not the tail. So, don't fret. Remember who you are and who you belong to when the cares of life start to make you feel insufficient and of no value. You must know you are destined to win! Regardless of your circumstances right now, it's not what it looks like.

It's not going to be like this always. People may revile you; they may overlook you, but they can't keep you down! They don't know who you really are. You are God's child—royalty. You are the head

Never, Never, Never Give Up!

and not the tail. You are above and not beneath. Stand firm; hold your head up and soar like an eagle.

Your joy is right around the corner.

Chapter 24

A Love That Never Fails

Love.
Some use it easily, tossing it around like an old, torn shoe.
Some say they love you when they have destroyed your self-esteem to pieces.
Some say they love you when they have given you fine clothes, furs, and diamonds.
Some say they love you when they want to persuade you to change your mind from right to wrong.
Have your lovers failed you?
I know a love that has never failed: the love of Jesus.

He loves us unconditionally with an everlasting love.
He gives us what we need.
He tells us in His word that when we are pressed down, He will strengthen and renew us.
Isaiah 40:29-31

Chapter 25

Where Am I?

How did I get to this point? It all started out with hitting and missing worship services. It got easier and easier for me to miss Sunday school, Bible class, and of course, prayer services. God became less and less apart of my life as I started lowering my standard, sporting gear I used to wear, hanging out at the old spot with old friends, and listening to music that didn't edify my soul.

I started picking up old habits while trying to convince myself that there wasn't anything wrong with what I was doing. I jumped into the deep; I was sinking in my old sinful ways.

Who was going to throw me a life jacket? Where would I go from here? I wasn't only missing in action (MIA), but I was a prisoner of war (POW), who had been captured by the enemy.

As I went down into the deep, I remembered the word of God: "Seek the Lord while he may be found; call on him while he is near."

Lord I'm calling unto You to let the wicked forsake his ways and saying that he will stop doing the things that displeases You. Allow them to repent of those things asking you for forgiveness.
I pray that You cleanse the righteous man from all unrighteousness, and let him return back to you Lord. Have mercy upon him. Pardon us of our sins.

If you are in need of help, reach out and receive the life jacket from the Lord. He'll come to your rescue when you find yourself lost.

So, where are? Are you MIA or a POW?

Chapter 26

It is Finished

St. John 19:30

It is finished really means it was the beginning. What does finished mean? Perfected, completed, ended. What was finished? Was it the sacrifice? Was it the betrayal? Or was it the denial.

Jesus finished what He was born to do. He was born to die for me, for you. What was finished on the cross was only the beginning for us. He died so we may live again. The Bible says Jesus was bruised for our iniquities, He was oppressed and afflicted, yet He opened not His mouth (Isaiah 53:5).

He could have called ten thousand angels, but He decided to die. He was taken from the living.

The Bible says He made his grave with the wicked; He had done no violence neither was deceit found in his mouth.

He did what He set out to do, although the human part had to go through the ridicule, the persecutions. His persecutors spat on Him. They beat Him and then laughed at Him.

Yet, we don't want to finish what God started in us. Why? Because of the suffering we must overcome. Its betrayal, its sacrifice, its denial come in different forms, but I say to you, my sisters and brothers, "Complete the process, so that God can say it is finished."

Go another step higher. Some of us want to get out of the process, but God is not through with us yet. We don't have our glorified bodies yet.

As long as we're in the flesh, there's a war going on in our flesh. The flesh wants to have its way. The Bible says every time we go to do good, evil is always present.

So when the game is against us, we must give it to the Heavenly Father. Then you'll find yourself rising to another level in God. You have to see the big picture. Don't run away from your situation; finish your course, and rise to the occasion! Your destiny awaits!

Evangelist Christine Dyer

Every time you are needed you are always there.

Very much a present help are your sincere prayers.

Answering the call of Christ to minister and intercede.

Never overlooking the hurting people needs.

Get up and go get' em attitude that you display.

Encouraging your brothers and sisters each and every day.

Lying still for the devil, no! That's simply not you.

Instead you trample over him for you have things to do.

Steadfast in your faith as you work for the Lord.

Teaching and training us how to properly use the sword.

Don't you ever forget how much, God has used you.

You just keep being faithful in the things that you do.

Example to me, Christine, you are in your walk.

Remembering your struggles and not just your talk.
Kimberly Reeves

PRAYER

Our Most Gracious God, I pray that you bless this reader. May every need be met, whether it be forgiveness, peace, love, joy or deliverance.

If there are precious souls that don't know you, I pray for their salvation. Open up their eyes to the Truth of the Word and open their ears to hear what You are speaking to their hearts. Let there be an obvious change in their lives.

Now, Father God, I pray that every word inside this book would encourage, empower and uplift the reader--In the name of Jesus. Thanks and Amen.

Acknowledgments

My publisher, Celesta Caston, for her hard work and patience.

My siblings and their spouses: Jeff & Gerry, Steve & Monica, Aaron & Kim, Frank & Jackie.

Cillastein, Scharlene, Shirlene for loving me as their big sister.

My other brothers, the Dyers, and their spouses (Nathan and Penny, Alvin and Michelle, Jerry and Emma).

Bill and Bruce for accepting me as their sister.

To my other mother, Vivian Delores Dyer, who taught me how to be a lady.

My Godparents: Jimmy & B Kelly, for financial and spiritual support.

My Godchildren: thanks for allowing me to be your Godmother.

The great leaders, Pastor Gregory C. Allen and Lady Ruby Allen, who were instrumental in teaching me how to apply the word of God in my life.

Bishop Keith T. Jenkins, my Pastor, teacher and mentor.

Lady Dollica Jenkins, a praying woman of God.

In memory of my father, Samuel Reeves; brother, Samuel Reeves Jr.; Bishop John S. Holly; and mother, Effie Holly; Pastor Robert C. Holly; Pastor

Barbara Ackerman; my dear friend, Aunt Georgia Cowan Purdue; Elder Shelly Robinson and Sister Regina Warren.

The Open Door Evangelistic World Ministry Church Family.

The powerful and anointed prayer intercessors, who cover me in prayer.

Sister Hattie B–thanks for sowing into my vision.

My prayer partners, far and near, for being on the wall of prayer and not coming down until God says so.

Pastor David Blair, Lady Blair, Lue M, Janie R, Ella J, Sandra J, Nakida G, Angela H, Luvenia S, Jennifer H, Shelly Lynn M, Penny K, Renee C, Lawanda C, C Wallace, Priscilla B, Yvette H, and Pastor Doris.

The Cowan Family (aunts and uncles) for love and support.

The Reeves and Dunklin Family (aunts &uncles) for love and support.

Aunt Rozenia—thanks for love & financial support.

My very good friend, Sharon Wade, who is very ill. Here is to the remembrance of the good times we shared.

My nieces, nephews, and cousins who show great respect for me.

My Godsisters, Debbie and Keisha.

Diane C. –a long time friend.

Kim R. –thanks for teaching me the ropes.

My beautician, Catt, who helps me to look my very best.

My co-workers: Dwight, who encourages me daily to complete my goals; and David, who lightens my work load.

Bernadette, who has always encouraged me to write, and soar above measures.

In memory of my granddaughter, Keyahjhnaa.

To all of my friends, far and near, thank God for you all!

ABOUT THE AUTHOR

Christine Reeves Dyer is an ordained Elder at Open Door Evangelistic World Ministries in Minneapolis, MN. She preaches and teaches the gospel across the country and abroad (as far as Africa).

She is also a known scriptwriter and stage director with over twenty years of experience. Christine's most recent work is a play entitled: Have *You Made Your Reservations Yet?* She uses drama as a ministry tool to witness and encourage the lost.

Christine is the wife of Ronald J. Dyer, Sr. of 34 years and is the mother of three: Latasha, Latreace, and Ronald Jr. She has nine grandchildren and is a God Mother to many.

You may visit her at www.evgcrdyer.com.

www.ingramcontent.com/pod-product-compliance
Lightning Source LLC
Chambersburg PA
CBHW031301290426
44109CB00012B/676